Animal TECH

FLIPPERS & FINS

Tessa Miller

full tilt PRESS

Flippers & Fins
Animal Tech

Full Tilt Press
42982 Osgood Road
Fremont, CA 94539
readfulltilt.com

Editorial Credits
Design and layout by Sara Radka
Edited by Renae Gilles
Copyedited by Kristin J. Russo

Image Credits
Flickr: NOAA PMEL, 31; Getty Images: cover, Blend Images RM, 41 (foreground), Cultura RF, 23 (left), 26, Flickr Open, 12, 30, Flickr RF, 17 (top), 18, 33, 45, duncan1890, 11 (top), Peter Macdiarmid, 21, Tim Whitby, 29 (bottom), Marco Garcia, 35 (foreground), LokFung, 41 (background), Image Source, 4, 24, iStockphoto, 7, 8, 9, 10 (bottom), 11 (bottom), 14, 15, 16 (top), 17 (bottom), 34 (top), 37, 38, 40 (bottom), 40 (top), background, Moment Open, 10 (top), Moment RF, 1, 13, 22 (right), 22 (left), 28 (right), 42, RooM RF, 19, Science Photo Library RF, 16 (bottom), Scott Olson, 39, Stocktrek Images, 36, Westend61, 20, Jonathan Wood, 25, Mike Coppola, 27; Newscom: MCT, 23 (right), Wolfgang Langenstrassen, 32, Visual via ZUMA Press, 43, 5, David Barrett/UPPA/UPPA/ZUMAPRESS, 29 (top); Pixabay: cover, The Digital Artist, 34 (bottom); Shutterstock: cover, Studio BKK, 35 (background), Lance Sagar, 6, BESTWEB, 44; Wikimedia: Internet Archive Book Images, 28 (left)

ISBN: 978-1-62920-737-7 (library binding)
ISBN: 978-1-62920-777-3 (eBook)

CONTENTS

Dolphins are among the
smartest animals on earth.

Submarines of the future might be shaped like ocean animals, such as rays.

INTRODUCTION

The earth's oceans are full of mysteries. Scientists think that 95 percent of the earth's oceans are unexplored. New animals and plants are discovered every day. Some ocean animals are as small as a grain of sand. Others are the largest animals on the planet. Many sea creatures have special abilities. These abilities help them survive and thrive deep underwater. People can learn a lot by studying these animals.

Nature often gives scientists and **engineers** new ideas. They can use these ideas to help solve problems and make **technology** better. This is called biomimicry. "Bio" means life. "Mimicry" means to copy something else. People have been mimicking underwater animals for hundreds of years. They still do today. From 16th-century ships to the military uniforms of the future, many fascinating technologies have been **inspired** by animals.

engineer: a person who plans and builds tools, machines, or structures

technology: tools and knowledge used to meet a need or solve a problem

inspire: to motivate or lead to a new idea, usually creative

FISH

GALLEONS

Mackerel are a type of fish that live in the ocean and travel in schools. A single school can have thousands of fish and stretch for miles.

In the 1500s, it took a crew of more than 80 people to sail a galleon.

Many hundreds of years ago, people didn't have advanced technology for travel. They couldn't drive a car or fly in an airplane. But they could take a sailing ship. In the 14th and 15th centuries, these ships were slow. It took months for a large sailing ship, such as a carrack, to cross the Atlantic Ocean. A round trip from Spain to the Bahamas could take up to 16 months on a carrack.

These ships were slow because they were huge and heavy. The bodies of the ships were wide and deep. They could carry a lot of **cargo**. But because they were so slow, they became targets for pirates. They also couldn't transport food items that might go bad, because trips took too long.

By the 1500s, people wanted to cross the Atlantic Ocean faster. Shipmakers were working hard to make better ships. They had to come up with a better **design**. In the end, they were inspired by fast-swimming fish from the ocean. This inspiration led to a fast-moving sailing ship—the galleon.

cargo: items for sale that are moved by a ship, plane, or truck

design: to make a plan by thinking about the purpose or use of something

LESSONS FROM NATURE

Shipmakers in England studied the body shapes of different fish. One fish they focused on was the mackerel. Mackerel can swim very fast. They are also able to move very precisely. Their bodies are shaped like a teardrop or a torpedo. They have a large, round head and body with a slender tail. Shipmakers realized this shape might work well for ships, too. They started to design a new ship. The body of the ship, called the hull, was shaped more like a mackerel. The shipmakers also looked at fish that swim in **reefs**. These fish have pointed noses. Shipmakers gave the ship a pointed front, called the prow.

Now shipmakers had a ship that was long, narrow, and very fast, like a mackerel. Its pointed prow let it cut through the water smoothly. They called this new ship the galleon, which means "little ship" or "armed ship."

Mackerel are very nutritious. They are an important food source for people around the world.

The galleon was important during the Age of Discovery (about 1450–1650). This was a time of world exploration—and sometimes war.

The British galleon's new design made it the fastest ship in the world. Because it was so light and fast, it was used as a guard for slower cargo ships. This saved cargo ships from being attacked by pirates. In the late 1500s, the galleon was used to carry cargo. It could make a round trip from Europe to South America very quickly. Because of the faster travel time, fruits and vegetables could be shipped across longer distances. Many people in Europe were able to buy produce, such as tomatoes, for the first time.

DID YOU KNOW?
Mackerels can swim up to 6.8 miles (11 kilometers) per hour. Olympic swimmer Michael Phelps's fastest swim was 6 miles (9.7 km) per hour.

reef: a ridge of rock, sand, or coral near the surface of the ocean

TECH IN ACTION

The mackerel's unique body inspired a better design for 15th-century battleships.

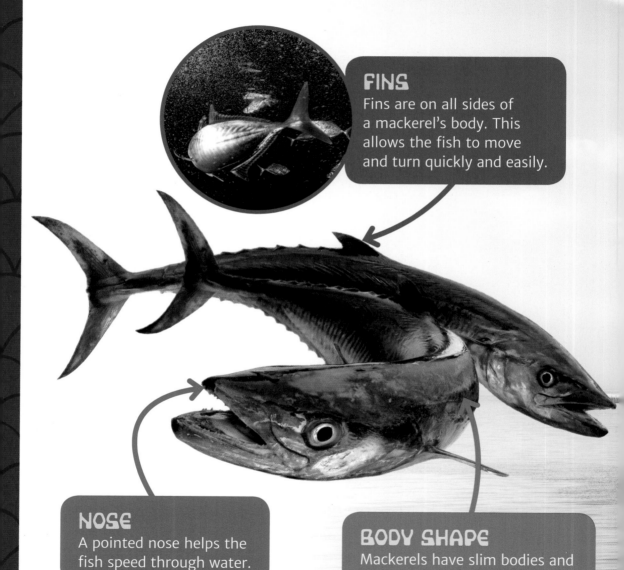

FINS
Fins are on all sides of a mackerel's body. This allows the fish to move and turn quickly and easily.

NOSE
A pointed nose helps the fish speed through water.

BODY SHAPE
Mackerels have slim bodies and a torpedo shape. They can swim very quickly in short bursts.

SAILS

The galleon's many sails helped it to out-maneuver other ships in battle.

PROW

The galleon's pointed prow let it cut through air and water.

HULL SHAPE

Galleons were long and narrow. They were shaped more like a fish than other ships during that time

SQUID

ELECTRICAL CIRCUITS

Squid have very complex eyes and brains. This makes them good hunters.

Electricity is a type of energy. Technology directs the flow of energy so it can be used to do work.

Every day, people depend on indicator lights. These lights show, or indicate, that tools and machines are working. Indicator lights tell people if a battery is charged. But what if the light does not work? What if a battery is dead, but the light does not respond? What if the light just flickers?

This can happen for two reasons. An electric signal can move too slowly. Then the light won't turn on or off when it's supposed to. Or there can be too much **noise**. This makes the electricity bounce back and forth. This causes the light to flicker. These issues can cause big problems for people who need machines to do their jobs, such as doctors.

Otto H. Schmitt was worried about failing indicator lights. In the 1930s, Schmitt was a student. He was studying electrical **circuits**. He hoped to design a new part for circuits. He wanted it to act as a better on/off switch. First he needed to find an electrical system with a good on/off switch. Then he could copy how it worked. So Schmitt started looking at nature. What he found was an animal with a complex electrical system in its body—the squid.

noise: random and unwanted electrical signals

circuit: a piece of technology that contains or directs a flow of electricity

LESSONS FROM NATURE

Many animals have complex **nervous systems**. One part of the nervous system is the axon. Axons are like threads or cables. They carry electrical signals around the body. Axons act as an on/off switch for the signals. In squids, axons are really big. They are also very strong. This lets scientists study them easily.

Nervous systems can have the same problems as indicator lights. Electrical signals can move too slowly. Or there can be too much noise. To solve these problems, squid axons set **thresholds**. First, the squid's brain sends a signal to a tentacle. The signal is a message for the tentacle to move. The signal travels through the axon. The electricity builds up. Then it crosses the threshold. Like an on/off switch, this **triggers** a response. The tentacle moves.

Electricity can move through the nervous system at more than 200 miles (320 km) per hour.

Every cell phone contains a circuit. The circuit powers all of the phone's functions.

Schmitt studied squid axons. He saw how their thresholds work. Then he invented a new part for electrical circuits. It is called the Schmitt trigger. It works just like a squid axon. It sets new thresholds. This turns electricity on and off at the right time. It also reduces noise. Today, the Schmitt trigger is used in millions of machines and electronics, including computers.

DID YOU KNOW?
People sometimes mistake squid for octopuses. Squid have triangle-shaped heads with two fins. Octopuses have round heads without fins. Both have blue blood.

nervous system: the system of body parts that directs electricity in the body to control movement and feeling

threshold: the point or level at which something happens

trigger: to cause something to start working

TECH IN ACTION

Otto Schmitt's study of the squid led to technology many people use every day.

NERVOUS SYSTEM

The squid's nervous system controls electricity in the body.

THRESHOLD

When energy in a squid axon crosses a threshold, it causes a reaction. This includes movement.

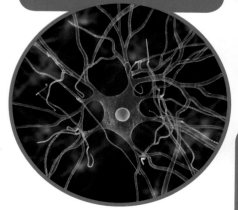

SOLUTION

Squid axons make good on/off switches and control noise. This lets a squid's body respond to messages from the brain quickly.

ELECTRICAL SYSTEM

Cables, circuits, and wires carry electricity around a computer.

TRIGGER

Schmitt triggers set new thresholds for electrical signals. Electricity has to cross the threshold. This triggers a reaction.

IMPROVEMENT

Schmitt triggers improve circuits. They reduce noise and act as on/off switches for important electrical signals.

WHALES

WIND TURBINES

A humpback whale has to eat thousands of pounds of food a day. This gives it the energy it needs to survive.

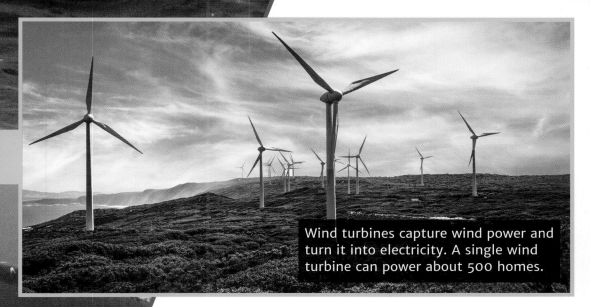

Wind turbines capture wind power and turn it into electricity. A single wind turbine can power about 500 homes.

A weak wind begins to blow. It crosses fields and hills, gaining strength. It was once a small gust. Now it's as fast as a train. Then, it reaches a wind farm. It blows through the towering white wind turbines. The blades of the wind turbines turn, harnessing the power of the wind and turning it into electricity.

This electricity is used to power homes and buildings. Right now, about 4 percent of the electricity used in the United States comes from wind power. Scientists want to raise this to 20 percent by 2030. To do this, they have to make windmills more **effective**.

The answer may have been found—not in the air, but in the water. A scientist named Frank Fish discovered that the flippers of humpback whales work like the blades of wind turbines. But the flippers have bumps called tubercles. They help humpback whales use their flippers more effectively.

effective: successful in achieving a desired effect or result

LESSONS FROM NATURE

To turn in tight circles, whales point their fins straight down. Swimming like this creates whirlpools along the flippers. This creates **drag**, which slows the whale down. But many large whales have tubercles. Tubercles allow water to flow over the flipper. This breaks up whirlpools before they even start. No whirlpools around the fins means less drag. Now the whale can swim smoothly. Without tubercles, large whales wouldn't be able to turn sharply enough to hunt for fish.

The humpback whale has tubercles along its two front fins. It also has them on its forehead, snout, and chin.

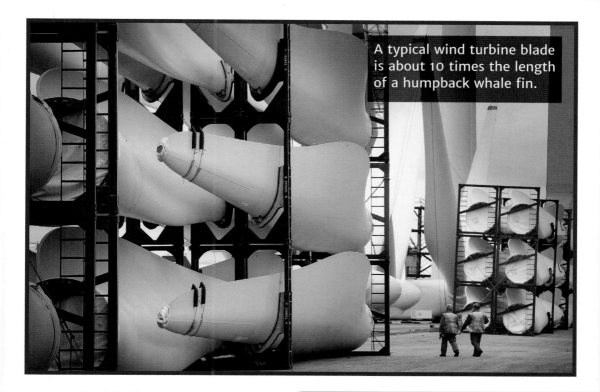

A typical wind turbine blade is about 10 times the length of a humpback whale fin.

Frank Fish discovered that tubercles work just as well in the air. **Engineers** are now putting them on fan blades. They can be used for small fans in homes and businesses. They can also be used for wind turbines. Tubercles on the blades help them spin in less wind. This makes them more efficient. The blades can be built smaller. But they are still just as powerful as larger blades. This saves money. It also means wind turbines can be put in more places, including cities.

DID YOU KNOW?

When hunting, a humpback whale swims in tight circles around a school of fish. The whale blows lots of tiny bubbles. The bubbles create a net that catches the fish. The whale then swallows them in one gulp.

drag: the force of water or air that pushes against something as it moves

engineer: a person who plans and builds tools, machines, or structures

TECH IN ACTION

Tubercles help a humpback whale move better in the water. They also help a fan blade move better in the air.

TUBERCLES
Flippers have tubercles on their front edges. These reduce drag.

SIZE
Humpback whale flippers are really big. They move through a lot of water.

GLIDING
Flippers are shaped like bird wings. The shape helps them glide through the water.

LENGTH

Wind turbine blades can be as long as a Boeing 747 plane. They move through a lot of air.

RIDGES

New blades have ridges cut into the front side. These increase efficiency.

CUTTING

A fan blade has a wing-like shape. This helps it cut through the air more smoothly.

SHARKS

SWIMSUITS

Great white sharks never stop swimming. It is part of how they breathe.

It is not unusual for Olympic swimmers to swim for two or three hours every day.

The whistle blows. A line of swimmers dives into the water. One swimmer is wearing a shiny gray swimsuit. Stroke for stroke, each swimmer is a powerful **competitor**. They are equally matched. Yet the swimmer in the gray suit is pulling ahead. She reaches the last lap. Finally she taps the wall. She finished seconds before the next swimmer. She has won the Olympic gold medal.

What is so special about her suit? Did it give her an edge over her competitors? Her suit was designed to work like a shark's skin. Much like a shark's skin, her suit helped her swim faster.

Sharks are the top **predators** of the oceans. To catch everything they need to eat, they have to be fast. A shark can swim 10 times faster than any human on record. Designers at the swimsuit company Speedo were looking to improve their swimsuits. It makes sense that they looked at sharks to design a new fabric.

competitor: someone who takes part in a sport or other pursuit to try to win

predator: an animal that hunts or eats other animals

LESSONS FROM NATURE

A shark's skin is unique. Each scale is shaped like a fang. It is rounded in the front and pointed in the back. These tiny ridges are called denticles. The denticles lie like feathers on wings. They overlap each other by a little bit. It is just enough to create a surface that bends and moves easily with the shark's movements.

The denticles act like tubercles on whale flippers. Whirlpools might form along a shark's body. Denticles break them up as the shark swims. This creates less drag. Less drag means a shark can swim quickly and smoothly.

Shark scales are not like fish scales. They are actually more like little teeth.

Speedo's most popular shark-inspired swimsuits cost at least $300.

Researchers at Speedo used these facts to make a new type of swimsuit. They called it Fastskin. Fastskin fabric is tight but flexible. It has denticles on the surface. The Fastskin swimsuit reduces drag up to 4 percent. This is a lot during a competition, when every second counts.

Engineers are also looking at shark skin. They are designing a material to coat the outside of planes and ships. Planes would be more **aerodynamic**. Ships would be more **hydrodynamic**. The special coating could save companies a lot of fuel. This would save money and help reduce pollution.

DID YOU KNOW?
Fastskin swimsuits weren't allowed after the 2008 Summer Olympics. Officials thought they gave swimmers an unfair edge over their competitors.

researcher: someone whose job is to study a topic in great detail

aerodynamic: able to move easily through air

hydrodynamic: able to move easily through water

TECH IN ACTION

Sharks are mighty predators of the deep. People have designed suits so they can swim more like sharks.

DENTICLES
The denticles on a shark's skin reduce its drag.

COVERING
Denticles cover every inch of a shark's body. They make the shark's skin more flexible.

SHAPE
Most sharks have long, slim bodies and pointed noses. This shape makes them very hydrodynamic.

FABRIC
The Fastskin swimsuit is covered in shark-like denticles.

FIT
The special fabric of the Fastskin suit makes the suit more flexible, so it molds to a swimmer's body.

FORM
The swimsuit is full length and stiff. This keeps a swimmer's shape long and slim.

DOLPHINS

TSUNAMI SENSORS

Dolphins and other large sea creatures move to deep water when there is a storm.

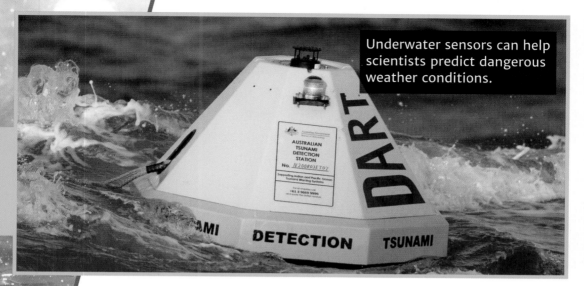

Underwater sensors can help scientists predict dangerous weather conditions.

An earthquake rumbles deep out in the ocean. Nobody is around to feel it. But the **tsunami** the quake produces will soon slam into land, destroying everything in its path.

Scientists are working on ways to better **detect** and predict these earthquakes and tsunamis. There are hundreds of tsunami sensors all over the earth's oceans. They are connected to buoys. Buoys are brightly colored objects that float and mark areas of water. Some buoys mark unsafe waters, but not all. And that's not what these bouys are doing. When there is an earthquake, a signal is sent from the sensor to a computer on the buoy. The signal goes to a **satellite**. Then it goes to a computer on land. Scientists then study the signal. This all takes a long time. Sometimes a signal is too confusing to figure out.

Scientists want to improve this technology. They are studying how dolphins **communicate**. Dolphins are able to send many sounds through the water. The sounds can travel long distances very quickly.

---

tsunami: a large wave from the ocean that causes destruction when it reaches land

detect: to notice something that is hard to see or hear

satellite: a man-made object that orbits the earth and is used to send data signals

communicate: to say or tell; to give information

LESSONS FROM NATURE

Deep-ocean Assessment and Reporting of Tsunami (DART) has a system of tsunami sensors that spans the globe.

Dolphins have a special way of communicating. They use many different chirps, tweets, and clicks. Dolphins send these sounds out at multiple **frequencies**. It's like playing one song on several radio stations at once. Sometimes a radio station gets a lot of static. But you can tune into another to keep listening to the song. The ocean is a noisy place. Dolphins can't always hear each other on a noisy frequency. So they listen to a different one. This lets dolphins talk without being interrupted. They can even communicate when the water gets rough and choppy.

For eight years, a team of researchers at EvoLogics in Germany studied dolphins. They wanted to see if they could mimic how dolphins communicate. They built a new sensor that uses dolphin-like sounds. When there is an earthquake, it sends signals across many frequencies. The sensor is now being tested in the Indian Ocean. The new technology seems to be giving off much clearer signals. It can let scientists predict natural events, such as tsunamis, sooner. This would give people more time to evacuate and save countless lives each year.

---

frequency: the rate at which a vibration occurs, such as the vibration of sound waves

Dolphins also blow bubbles, move their jaws, and touch fins to communicate.

TECH IN ACTION

By mimicking dolphin calls, people are improving tsunami warning systems in multiple ways.

CHATTER
Dolphins use chirps, tweets, and clicks to talk to each other.

DISTANCE
Dolphin calls travel up to 15.5 miles (25 km) underwater.

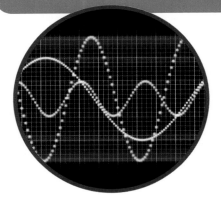

CLEAR
Even in rough seas, dolphin calls are not confused with other sounds.

NOISES

New sonar systems use a range of frequencies to send signals and communicate with satellites.

UNDERSTANDABLE

The new signals are clear and easy for scientists to understand.

RANGE

Signals travel through 11 miles (18 km) of water from the ocean floor.

CEPHALOPODS

CAMOUFLAGE

Cephalopods, such as octopuses, have no bones. They can lie very flat. They can also fit through tiny spaces.

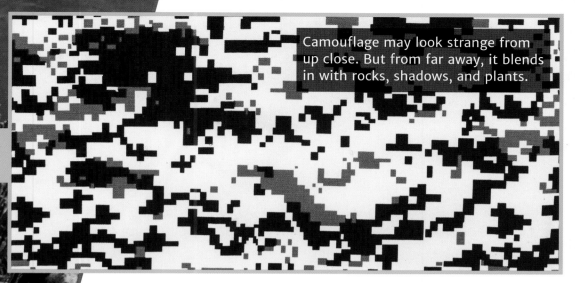

Camouflage may look strange from up close. But from far away, it blends in with rocks, shadows, and plants.

An orange-and-red octopus swims through calm waters. Settling on the sandy bottom, it stretches out eight limbs. Each one digs in the sand, looking for food. Just as a tentacle grasps a clam, the octopus freezes. It looks up. There is a dark shape moving through the water. Slowly, the octopus pulls its limbs back. The color of its skin begins to change. Now it matches the brown and gray of the sand and rocks around it. The dark shape, a seal, passes over. **Camouflage** has saved the octopus from becoming dinner.

To survive, cephalopods have to be sneaky. These are ocean animals with large heads and long arms. They include octopus, squid, and cuttlefish. Many cephalopods have a special trick. Cephalopods can change color. They can then match their **environment**. This lets them hide wherever they want. Camouflage lets cephalopods blend into rocks or coral. Other animals use camouflage. Green insects can look like leaves. Fish can look like sand on the ocean floor. But only certain animals can change their colors as they move.

camouflage: a way of hiding by blending in with your surroundings

environment: the air, water, plants, animals, weather, and other things in an area

LESSONS FROM NATURE

Cephalopods have three layers of skin. Each layer of skin has different color **pigments**. Beneath the skin is a layer of muscle. The muscles act as a trigger. This changes the colors in the skin layers.

Researchers across the US are working together. They are creating a new type of fabric. This fabric changes colors much like a cephalopod's skin. So far, researchers have been able to make a three-layer fabric. It can change from black to white. The first layer is made up of tiny light sensors. The next layer has small motors. The last layer is made up of color **capsules**. First the sensors read a color change in the surrounding environment. Then the motors turn on. They trigger the color capsules. The capsules then change from black to white. This is an important first step in making color-changing fabric.

Cuttlefish use camouflage to hide from predators, such as dolphins. Cuttlefish might also change their colors to communicate.

Camouflage protects soldiers and their equipment from enemies.

Scientists are now working to improve this technology. They want to make fabric that can change to any color. The military could use the fabric to design a set of camouflage for every soldier. Car designers want to use it for car paints. In an emergency, ambulances and police cars could change to brighter colors. This would make them more visible to other drivers.

DID YOU KNOW?
During World Word I (1914–1918) some ships were painted with zebra stripes. This type of camouflage breaks up the zebra's outline, hiding it from predators. In the same way, the stripes helped hide ships from enemies.

pigment: a substance that changes the color of something

capsule: a small container, usually round or cylindrical

TECH IN ACTION

Many animals use color-changing camouflage.
Soon humans will, too, thanks to biomimicry.

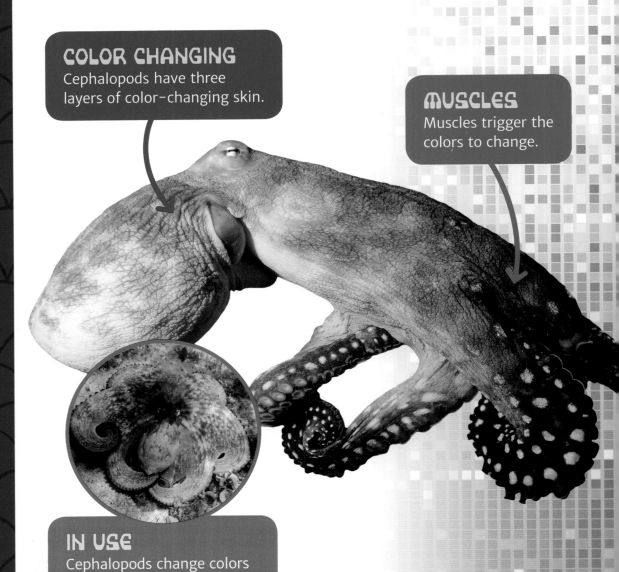

COLOR CHANGING
Cephalopods have three
layers of color-changing skin.

MUSCLES
Muscles trigger the
colors to change.

IN USE
Cephalopods change colors
to match their environment.
They can hide in plain sight.

COLOR SWITCHING
Scientists have designed a fabric that changes from black to white.

MOTORS
Tiny motors trigger color capsules to change colors.

FUTURE USE
One day, the fabric may be used for military uniforms. Uniforms would change color as soldiers move through different environments.

FLIPPERS & FINS

CONCLUSION

Biomimicry of whales has also led to a new water filter. It mimics how humpback and blue whales filter-feed.

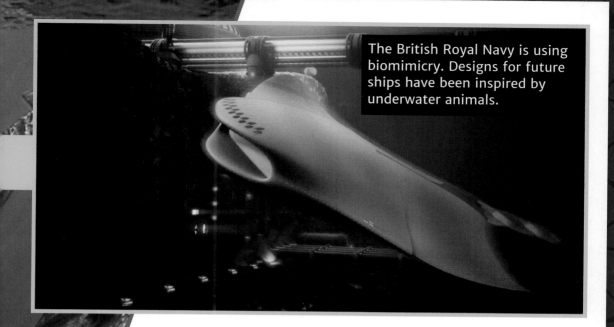

The British Royal Navy is using biomimicry. Designs for future ships have been inspired by underwater animals.

There are hundreds of thousands of different types of creatures in the oceans. Many more are waiting to be discovered. Scientists look to the ocean every day for inspiration. This inspiration leads technology in new directions.

For a long time, people did not realize just how intelligent dolphins are. But now researchers have studied how they communicate. Scientists have mimicked dolphin chirps and clicks to build better tsunami sensors. **Biologists** continue to study dolphin communication. They hope to someday use these chirps and clicks to have conversations with dolphins.

In the past, galleons were made faster because of biomimicry. Shipbuilders copied fish. Now shipbuilders are designing new submarines. The submarines don't use propellers to move forward. They have flippers and fins to move like whales.

People continue to look deep into the oceans for inspiration. You never know what will be found next.

---

biologist: someone who studies living things, such as plants and animals

ACTIVITY

MAKE YOUR OWN CAMOUFLAGE

Have you ever wondered how animals can hide in plain sight? Many do it with camouflage. With this activity, you can design your own camouflage shirt to wear.

WHAT YOU NEED

- large T-shirt
- fabric markers and/or paints
- fabric glue
- scraps of natural-colored materials, such as streamers, crepe paper, newsprint, tissue paper, etc.
- scissors
- paper and pencils

WHAT TO DO

1. Break into groups. Assign each group a specific area to blend into. The area can be grass, trees, bushes, rocks, or dirt.

2. With your group, look closely at your environment. Make a list of all the colors you see. Look for different shapes and textures. Make a list of what you see.

3. Sketch out what you want your shirt to look like. Check your list of colors, shapes, and textures.

4. Build your camouflage shirt. Cut shapes out of the natural-colored materials. Glue them to the shirt. You can also use fabric markers and paints to mimic the colors and shapes in your environment.

5. Once the shirt is done (and dry if paints are used), try it out. Have one group member put it on. Have them hide in their environment. The other groups can then try to find them.

6. Afterward, think about what made it hard to find people. What made it easy to find them? What would you change to make your camouflage shirt better?

GLOSSARY

aerodynamic: able to move easily through air

biologist: someone who studies living things, such as plants and animals

camouflage: a way of hiding by blending in with your surroundings

capsule: a small container, usually round or cylindrical

cargo: items for sale that are moved by a ship, plane, or truck

circuit: a piece of technology that contains or directs a flow of electricity

communicate: to say or tell; to give information

competitor: someone who takes part in a sport or other pursuit to try to win

design: to make a plan by thinking about the purpose or use of something

detect: to notice something that is hard to see or hear

drag: the force of water or air that pushes against something as it moves

effective: successful in achieving a desired effect or result

engineer: a person who plans and builds tools, machines, or structures

engineer: a person who plans and builds tools, machines, or structures

environment: the air, water, plants, animals, weather, and other things in an area

frequency: the rate at which a vibration occurs, such as the vibration of sound waves

hydrodynamic: able to move easily through water

inspire: to motivate or lead to a new idea, usually creative

nervous system: the system of body parts that directs electricity in the body to control movement and feeling

noise: random and unwanted electrical signals

pigment: a substance that changes the color of something

predator: an animal that hunts or eats other animals

reef: a ridge of rock, sand, or coral near the surface of the ocean

researcher: someone whose job is to study a topic in great detail

satellite: a man-made object that orbits the earth and is used to send data signals

technology: tools and knowledge used to meet a need or solve a problem

threshold: the point or level at which something happens

trigger: to cause something to start working

tsunami: a large wave from the ocean that causes destruction when it reaches land

READ MORE

Fleming, Candace. *Papa's Mechanical Fish.* New York: Margaret Ferguson Books, 2013.

Holzweiss, Kristina. *Amazing Makerspace DIY with Electricity.* New York: Children's Press, 2018.

Jenkins, Steve and Robin Page. *Flying Frogs and Walking Fish: Leaping Lemurs, Tumbling Toads, Jet-Propelled Jellyfish, and More Surprising Ways That Animals Move.* Boston: Houghton Mifflin Harcourt, 2016.

Kelsey, Elin. *Wild Ideas: Let Nature Inspire Your Thinking.* Berkeley, Calif.: Owlkids Books, Inc., 2015.

Mara, Wil. *From Sharks to . . . Swimsuits.* Innovations from Nature. Ann Arbor, Mich.: Cherry Lake Publishing, 2013.

WEBSITES

https://www.loc.gov/rr/scitech/mysteries/biomimicry.html
Read more about the mysteries of biomimicry.

https://www.sciencenewsforstudents.org/article/cool-jobs-science-deep-beneath-waves
Read about the jobs of scientists studying the ocean.

http://thekidshouldseethis.com/post/mimicking-shark-skin-to-combat-superbugs-bacteria-biomimicry
Watch a video on shark skin biomimicry.

https://kids.nwf.org/Home/Kids/Ranger-Rick/Animals/Fish/Creeps-Deep.aspx
See some of the ocean's strangest fish.

https://vimeo.com/channels/asknaturenuggets/50725958
Watch a video about octopus.

INDEX